A TRUE BOOK™

My United States

Louisiana

JENNIFER ZEIGER

Children's Press®
An Imprint of Scholastic Inc.

Content Consultant
James Wolfinger, PhD, Associate Dean and Professor
College of Education, DePaul University, Chicago, Illinois

Library of Congress Cataloging-in-Publication Data
Names: Zeiger, Jennifer, author.
Title: Louisiana / by Jennifer Zeiger.
Description: New York, NY : Children's Press, an imprint of Scholastic Inc., 2018. | "A True Book." | Includes bibliographical
    references and index.
Identifiers: LCCN 2017000112| ISBN 9780531252574 (library binding : alk. paper) | ISBN 9780531232873 (pbk. : alk. paper)
Subjects: LCSH: Louisiana—Juvenile literature.
Classification: LCC F369.3 .Z45 2018 | DDC 976.3—dc23
LC record available at https://lccn.loc.gov/2017000112

Photographs ©: cover: Photononstop/Superstock, Inc.; back cover ribbon: AliceLiddelle/Getty Images; back cover bottom:
Imke Lass/Redux; 3 bottom: Jerry "Woody"/Flickr; 3 map: Jim McMahon; 4 left: reptiles4all/Shutterstock; 4 right: togmit/
iStockphoto; 5 bottom: Science Source; 5 top: Peter Unger/Getty Images; 6 top: haydens/Stockimo/Alamy Images; 7 center:
f11photo/Shutterstock; 7 bottom: Gary Fowler/Shutterstock; 7 top: Neala McCarten/Alamy Images; 8-9: Rigoulet Gilles/hemis.
fr/Getty Images; 11: Danita Delimont/Alamy Images; 12: Brandy McKnight/Shutterstock; 13: Wesley Bocxe/The Image Works;
14: Lindsay Helms/Shutterstock; 15: imageBROKER/Superstock, Inc.; 16-17: Ian Dagnall/Alamy Images; 19: Gerald Herbert/AP
Images; 20: Tigatelu/Dreamstime; 22 left: YAY Media AS/Alamy Images; 22 right: Brothers Good/Shutterstock; 23 top right:
NaturePL/Superstock, Inc.; 23 bottom left: togmit/iStockphoto; 23 top center: Robert Anderson/Alamy Images; 23 bottom center:
Eudyptula/iStockphoto; 23 top left: digitalr/iStockphoto; 23 bottom right: reptiles4all/Shutterstock; 24-25: National Geographic
Creative/Alamy Images; 27: The News-Star, Margaret Croft/AP Images; 29: Howard Pyle/The Granger Collection; 30: National
Geographic Creative/Alamy Images; 31 top right: Science Source; 31 top left: YAY Media AS/Alamy Images; 31 bottom left:
Howard Pyle/The Granger Collection; 31 bottom right: Wesley Bocxe/The Image Works; 32: Saul Loeb/Getty Images; 33: Science
Source; 34-35: Ray Laskowitz/Getty Images; 36: Stephen Lew/Cal Sports Media/Alamy Images; 37: Cheryl Gerber/Getty Images;
38: John Moore/Getty Images; 39: Joe Baraban/Alamy Images; 40 bottom: caelmi/iStockphoto; 40 background: PepitoPhotos/
iStockphoto; 41: Peter Unger/Getty Images; 42 top left: The Granger Collection; 42 bottom left: Michael Ochs Archives/Getty
Images; 42 top right: Granamour Weems Collection/Alamy Images; 42 center right: Underwood Photo Archives/Superstock,
Inc.; 42 bottom right: AGIP - Rue des Archives/The Granger Collection; 43 top left: Marty Heitner/The Image Works; 43 top right:
s_bukley/Shutterstock; 43 center left: Food Network/Everett Collection; 43 center right: Tinseltown/Shutterstock; 43 bottom left:
Stacy Revere/Getty Images; 43 bottom center: Frazer Harrison/Getty Images; 43 bottom right: ZUMA Press, Inc./Alamy Images;
44 center: Jim West/Alamy Images; 44 bottom: graphiknation/iStockphoto; 45 top: John Moore/Getty Images; 45 bottom:
National Geographic Creative/Alamy Images; 45 center: Brandy McKnight/Shutterstock.

Maps by Map Hero, Inc.

**Front cover: A horse-drawn carriage in
the French Quarter of New Orleans**

**Back cover: A houseboat in
Atchafalaya Swamp**

Welcome to Louisiana

Find the Truth!

Everything you are about to read is true **except** for one of the sentences on this page.

Which one is **TRUE**?

T or F Louisiana is broken into parishes rather than counties.

T or F French explorers were the first people to settle in what is now Louisiana.

Find the answers in this book.

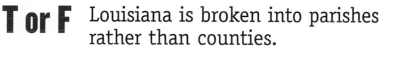

UNITED STATES

Louisiana

Contents

THE BIG TRUTH!

Magnolia

What Represents Louisiana?

Alligator

Historic French Quarter

3 History

How did Louisiana become
the state it is today?

4 Culture

What do Louisianans do for work and fun?

Jazz legend
Louis Armstrong is
from New Orleans.

This Is Louisiana!

1 Kisatchie National Forest

Established in 1930, this is Louisiana's only national forest. Visitors can hike, swim, and camp as they enjoy woodland views.

ARKANSAS

SHREVEPORT

Driskill Mountain

MONROE

Poverty Point National Monument

Toledo Bend Reservoir

Red

Black

Mississippi

NATCHITOCHES

Kisatchie National Forest

1

ALEXANDRIA

LOUISIANA

TEXAS

Calcasieu

Atchafalaya

MISSISSIPPI

2 Old State Capitol Museum

Bourbon

The Causeway

Lake Pontchartrain

Sabine

The Cajun Prairie

Evangeline Oak Tree

BATON ROUGE

4

SLIDELL

LAKE CHARLES

Frog Festival

LAFAYETTE

Historic French Quarter

3

NEW ORLEANS

Mardi Gras festival

Intracoastal

Waterway

Jazz Fest

Mississippi

Atchafalaya Swamp

Atchafalaya Bay

Mississippi River and Delta

N W E S

0   60
Miles

Gulf of Mexico

GULF OF MEXICO

② Old State Capitol Museum

Located in Baton Rouge, this remarkable building was once the center of Louisiana's government. Today, it is a museum honoring the state's rich history and culture.

③ New Orleans French Quarter

The most famous neighborhood in New Orleans, the French Quarter, is also the city's oldest. This is a great place to visit for anyone interested in architecture. At the neighborhood's center, Bourbon Street offers a range of music, food, and markets.

④ Lake Pontchartrain

Lake Pontchartrain is a vast lake in southwestern Louisiana. Crossing the lake is the Lake Pontchartrain Causeway. Its twin 24-mile-long (39-kilometer) bridges are the world's longest over water.

Louisiana has more than 3 million acres (1.2 million hectares) of wetlands.

CHAPTER 1

Land and Wildlife

What comes to mind when you think of Louisiana? Is it the famous city of New Orleans, with its brightly colored parades and vibrant music scene? How about hungry alligators floating across a steamy swamp? Or maybe it's somebody speaking Louisiana **Creole**? This language, with elements of French and various African languages, is rarely spoken outside of Louisiana. Creole is just one of many things that make Louisiana unique, a state that combines its French heritage with diverse cultures in a subtropical setting.

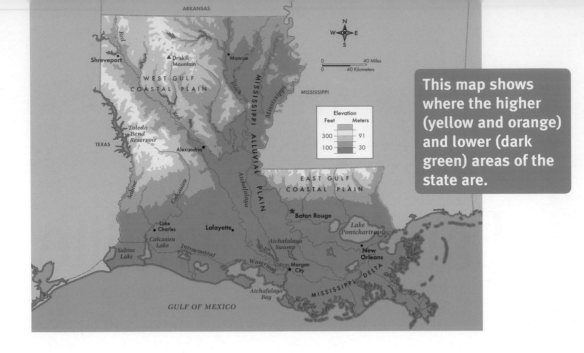

This map shows where the higher (yellow and orange) and lower (dark green) areas of the state are.

Water, Water, Everywhere

There's no denying that Louisiana is a wet place. There's water in the rivers, the lakes, the **bayous** along the Gulf of Mexico, and even the air. The Mississippi River runs south through the center of the state. Low-lying **floodplains** lie along the river's sides. A **silt**-filled **delta** forms where the Mississippi empties into the Gulf of Mexico. Around the delta region are vast areas of wetlands, where water covers much of the soil throughout the year.

Atchafalaya Swamp

The Atchafalaya River runs south through Louisiana and empties into the Gulf of Mexico. The bustling and beautiful Atchafalaya Basin is found around the river's delta. This region covers about 1 million acres (400,000 ha), making it the United States' largest river swamp. Visitors can take boat tours to explore the basin's vast cypress forest and look for its countless animals.

Louisiana's highest point, Driskill Mountain, is located in the northwestern part of the state.

Lows and Highs

Louisiana's coastal areas and floodplains are generally close to sea level. Some areas are even below sea level. But the land there isn't underwater. How is this possible? The area is shaped like a bowl. Right at the coastline, the land sits at sea level. It then rises slightly before dipping back down. Louisiana isn't all lowlands, though. The northwestern part of the state is full of hills and bluffs.

What's the Weather?

Louisiana mostly stays warm all year and has a lot of rain. Winters rarely dip toward freezing. Summers can be very hot, with temperatures often rising above 90 degrees Fahrenheit (32 degrees Celsius) with high **humidity**. Summer is also hurricane season. Hurricanes are intense storms that develop over the ocean. If they hit land, they bring severe wind, rain, and flooding.

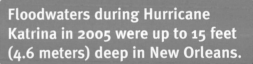

MAXIMUM TEMPERATURE	MINIMUM TEMPERATURE
114°F	-16°F

Floodwaters during Hurricane Katrina in 2005 were up to 15 feet (4.6 meters) deep in New Orleans.

In 2005, Hurricane Katrina killed 1,577 people in Louisiana.

Though it looks like part of a tree, Spanish moss is a separate plant that grows in tree branches and hangs down.

Plant Life

Nearly half of Louisiana is covered in forest. In the northern hills, oak, beech, black walnut, and spruce pines grow. Farther south are live oaks covered in garlands of Spanish moss. Cypress trees fill the state's wetlands. Magnolia and dogwood trees grow throughout the state and boast colorful flowers. A range of grasses fill the state's prairie regions.

Louisiana Creatures

Alligators are perhaps the most famous Louisiana wetland residents. Catfish, crawfish, turtles, and oysters are also found in the state's many waters. Mammals such as otters, beavers, and raccoons call the wetlands home. So do herons, egrets, and the once-**endangered** brown pelican. In the state's forests are deer, rabbits, muskrats, opossums, and other furry creatures. Quail, turkeys, and ducks are found throughout Louisiana.

Beavers are the largest rodents in North America.

Louisiana's state capitol building is the tallest in the country.

CHAPTER 2

Government

Louisiana's capital, Baton Rouge, is located directly on the Mississippi River. Baton Rouge has been the home base of Louisiana's state government since 1879. This is where the state's elected officials gather to create new laws and carry out the government's many responsibilities. These leaders come from all over Louisiana, each representing a different part of the state.

Executive Branch

Like other U.S. states, Louisiana has three branches of government. Each has its own powers and responsibilities. The state's executive branch carries out, or enforces, Louisiana's laws. The head of this branch is the governor. The legislative branch creates the state's laws. It is made up of a 39-member Senate and a 105-member House of Representatives. The judicial branch interprets the state's laws. Louisiana's judges and lawyers work as part of this branch.

LOUISIANA'S STATE GOVERNMENT

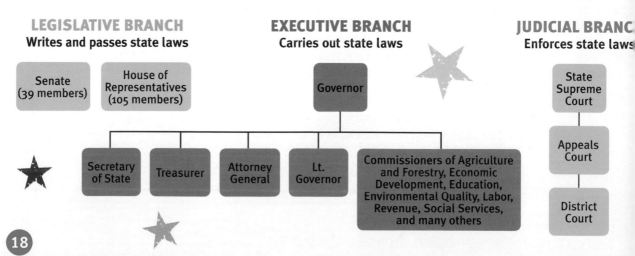

LEGISLATIVE BRANCH
Writes and passes state laws

- Senate (39 members)
- House of Representatives (105 members)

EXECUTIVE BRANCH
Carries out state laws

- Governor
  - Secretary of State
  - Treasurer
  - Attorney General
  - Lt. Governor
  - Commissioners of Agriculture and Forestry, Economic Development, Education, Environmental Quality, Labor, Revenue, Social Services, and many others

JUDICIAL BRANCH
Enforces state laws

- State Supreme Court
- Appeals Court
- District Court

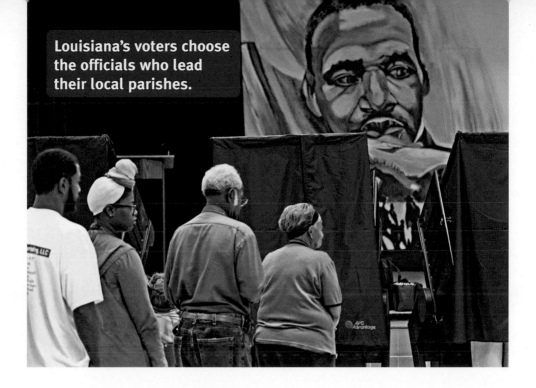

Louisiana's voters choose the officials who lead their local parishes.

All About Parishes

Louisiana is divided into 64 smaller sections called parishes. Parishes are a lot like the counties in other states. Each one has its own local government. Some are led by officials called commissioners. Others have police juries, which are run by elected officials called jurors. Despite their name, these groups aren't connected with police departments.

Louisiana in the National Government

Each state sends officials to represent it in the U.S. Congress. Like every state, Louisiana has two senators. The U.S. House of Representatives relies on a state's population to determine its numbers. Louisiana has six representatives in the House.

Every four years, states vote on the next U.S. president. Each state is granted a number of electoral votes based on its number of members of Congress. With two senators and six representatives, Louisiana has eight electoral votes.

2 senators and 6 representatives

8 electoral votes

With eight electoral votes, Louisiana's voice in presidential elections is about average.

Representing Louisiana

Elected officials in Louisiana represent a population with a range of interests, lifestyles, and backgrounds.

Ethnicity (2015 estimates)

1.8%
Asian

5.0%
Hispanic or Latino

1.6%
Two or more races

0.1%
Native Hawaiian and other Pacific Islander alone

0.8%
Native American or Alaska Native

Caucasian — **59.1%**

African American — **32.5%**

23% of the population have a degree beyond high school.

2/3 own their own homes.

73% live in cities.

4% of Louisianans were born in other countries.

83% of the population graduated from high school.

9% speak a language other than English at home.

What Represents Louisiana?

States choose specific animals, plants, and objects to represent the values and characteristics of the land and its people. Find out why these symbols were chosen to represent Louisiana or discover surprising curiosities about them.

Seal

The state seal is included on legal and government documents to show they are official. Louisiana's seal shows an eastern brown pelican feeding its young. Around this image is the state motto: "Union, Justice, Confidence."

Flag

Louisiana has had four different flags over the years. Its current flag was adopted in 1912. The flag simply shows the state seal on a blue background.

Crawfish

STATE CRUSTACEAN

Looking much like a tiny lobster, the crawfish is a favorite food for many Louisianans.

Bald Cypress

STATE TREE

Found in Louisiana's wetland areas, this tree has been an official state symbol since 1963.

Eastern Brown Pelican

STATE BIRD

Louisiana is nicknamed the Pelican State after this remarkable sea bird.

Magnolia

STATE FLOWER

This beautiful white flower grows on magnolia trees throughout Louisiana.

Catahoula Leopard Dog

STATE DOG

The catahoula leopard dog is the only dog breed to have originated in Louisiana.

Alligator

STATE REPTILE

Alligators are a common sight throughout Louisiana's many swamps and other wetlands.

Caddo people built homes using grass and other natural materials.

CHAPTER 3

History

Millions of years ago, dinosaurs and other prehistoric creatures roamed the land that is now Louisiana. Scientists have discovered the fossils of many ancient creatures throughout the state. These include dinosaurs, 30-million-year-old sharks, woolly **mammoths**, and huge sea reptiles called mosasaurs.

Louisiana's Native People

At an ancient settlement called Poverty Point, people of the ancient Woodland culture built huge mounds and earthen structures in a site larger than three football fields. The group lived or worked there between about 1800 and 1400 BCE.

In about 500 BCE, the Chitimacha settled in the delta region. Later, the Natchez arrived farther north along the Mississippi River. The Caddo settled in the northern hills, and other groups, such as the Choctaw and Bayogoula, moved into the region.

This map shows the general areas where Native American groups settled.

Many of the people who lived in the hills and plains of northern Louisiana were hunter-gatherers. They moved from place to place, hunting animals and gathering herbs, fruits, and vegetables. Groups who lived in the rich delta or swampy region to the south were farmers. The land there was much better for raising crops. Their settlements were often more permanent.

Europeans in Louisiana

Europe took no interest in what is now the state of Louisiana until 1682. That year, France's René-Robert Cavelier, Sieur de La Salle, traveled down the Mississippi River to its mouth at the Gulf of Mexico. La Salle claimed all the land around the river for France. He named it Louisiana, after France's King Louis XIV. The French tried to **colonize** the territory for decades. But they failed due to disease, poor crops, and conflicts with the native peoples.

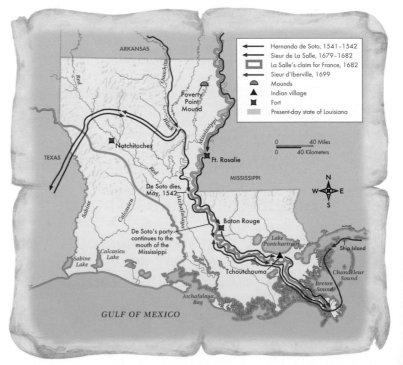

This map shows the routes taken by European explorers in the 1500s and 1600s.

ARKANSAS

Ouachita

Red

Black

Poverty Point Mound

Hernando de Soto, 1541–1542
Sieur de La Salle, 1679–1682
La Salle's claim for France, 1682
Sieur d'Iberville, 1699
Mounds
Indian village
Fort
Present-day state of Louisiana

0   40 Miles
0   40 Kilometers

Natchitoches

TEXAS

Mississippi

Ft. Rosalie

MISSISSIPPI

N
W   E
S

De Soto dies, May, 1542

Red

Calcasieu

Atchafalaya

Baton Rouge

Lake Pontchartrain

Ship Island

De Soto's party continues to the mouth of the Mississippi

Sabine

Sabine Lake

Calcasieu Lake

Tchoutchouma

Chandeleur Sound

Breton Sound

Atchafalaya Bay

GULF OF MEXICO

René-Robert Cavelier, Sieur de La Salle, claims Louisiana for France.

In 1718, France finally succeeded in creating a colony called New Orleans at the southern tip of the territory. Farms there flourished. The colony's port on the Mississippi River drew traders. But in the early 1800s, France went to war in Europe. To pay for this conflict, France sold New Orleans and the vast Louisiana Territory to the United States for $15 million in 1803.

Becoming a State

The land the United States gained in the Louisiana Purchase covered roughly 828,000 square miles (2,144,510 square km). Much of it was wilderness at the time. However, New Orleans and the surrounding area were a valuable center of trade and farming. In 1812, this area became the 18th U.S. state, taking the name Louisiana from the larger area of land to which it once belonged.

Timeline of Louisiana Events

2000 BCE
People arrive in the Louisiana area for the first time.

1800 BCE
The people of the Woodland culture settle at Poverty Point.

1718
New Orleans is founded.

2000 BCE → 1800 BCE → 1682 CE → 1718

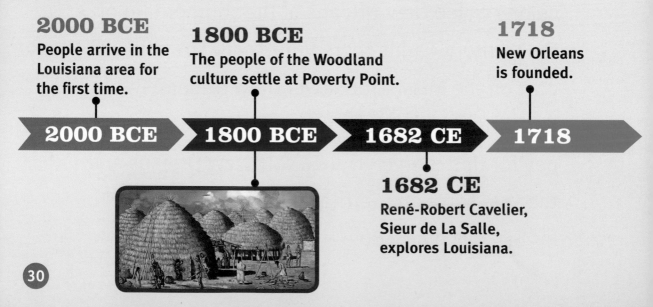

1682 CE
René-Robert Cavelier, Sieur de La Salle, explores Louisiana.

Changes and Challenges

Immigrants poured into the new state of Louisiana. Many were from France and its colonies. One group of colonists came from Canada. They became known as Cajuns. The British had forced them to leave Canada in the late 1700s.

Other Louisianans also came to the state against their will. By 1850, about half of the state's residents were slaves. Most of them worked on **plantations**.

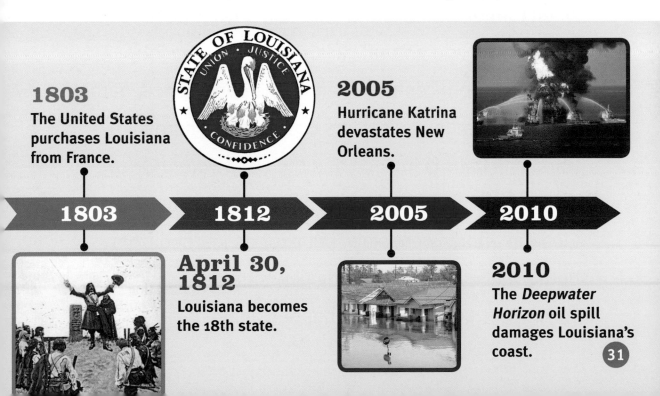

1803
The United States purchases Louisiana from France.

2005
Hurricane Katrina devastates New Orleans.

1803 — 1812 — 2005 — 2010

April 30, 1812
Louisiana becomes the 18th state.

2010
The *Deepwater Horizon* oil spill damages Louisiana's coast.

31

A pelican is covered with oil after the *Deepwater Horizon* disaster. Many animals died as a result of the oil spill.

Louisiana's economy suffered after the Civil War, when former slaves found little fair, paying work. Logging, oil, and natural gas brought in some jobs during the 20th century. Then, in the early 2000s, natural and environmental disasters caused great hardship. Hurricane Katrina in 2005 and the *Deepwater Horizon* oil spill in 2010 severely damaged the state's coastal areas. Cleanup efforts were slow, but experts learned from both events. They are putting new safeguards in place so similar tragedies do not happen again.

Bringing Jazz to the World

Louis Armstrong was born in New Orleans in 1901. As a child, he often sang on street corners. In his teens, he began learning to play the cornet, which is similar to a trumpet. Much of his knowledge came from listening to jazz bands performing in the city. Soon, he was playing in bands himself. He went on to perform around the world and even act in films. His unique voice and musical talent continue to influence artists today.

CHAPTER 4

Culture

In its long history, people from all over the world have moved into Louisiana. They brought their own foods, music, celebrations, stories, and languages. One place this melting pot of ideas is clear is in local music. Cajun and zydeco music often have lyrics in a form of French unique to Cajun communities. New Orleans's loose style of jazz is a combination of African, Creole, and other types of music.

Having Fun

Football is a big sport in Louisiana. The New Orleans Saints are the state's beloved pro team, while college teams such as those from Louisiana State University and Louisiana Tech also draw huge crowds to their games. Many of Louisiana's young athletes practice hard in hopes of playing for one of these teams.

Golf and basketball are other popular sports among Louisianans. With so many bodies of water, the state is also a great place to go fishing.

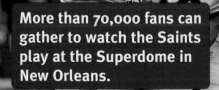

More than 70,000 fans can gather to watch the Saints play at the Superdome in New Orleans.

Born on the Bayou

People in Louisiana know how to enjoy themselves. If you like jazz, traditional Cajun music, or just about any other kind of music, you'll find live performances everywhere you look. Each year, people hold Mardi Gras

The first Mardi Gras celebration was held in 1699.

celebrations all around the state. Mardi Gras ("fat Tuesday" in French) was brought to Louisiana from France in colonial times. It is celebrated with parades and parties. Later in the season, New Orleans hosts the Jazz and Heritage Festival, where local musicians and world-famous stars alike perform for huge crowds.

At Work

Oil and natural gas form a big part of Louisiana's economy. The state's lush forests provide lumber. Agriculture is also important. Louisiana's warm, wet climate is perfect for growing sugarcane. Cotton, corn, and rice also thrive. Louisiana sells more than 1 billion pounds (454 million kilograms) of fish and shellfish each year.

These big businesses aren't the state's top employers, however. Most residents work in schools, research, transportation, or other service industries.

Louisiana fishers sell 10 percent of all the seafood produced in the United States, and the most shrimp of any state.

Oil Technology

Louisiana's first successful oil well was built in 1901. The well extended less than 2,000 feet (610 m) into the ground. Technology has changed significantly since then, and wells can reach much farther underground. In the mid-20th century, innovators created a way to access the oil that lies below the ocean floor. This led to a revolution in offshore drilling. Today, drills routinely reach more than 20,000 feet (6,096 m) into the ground and as deep as 8,000 feet (2,438 m) into the water.

A Louisiana Feast

Louisiana's mix of cultures has produced a range of sauces, spices, and stews. Two of the state's most famous dishes are gumbo and jambalaya. Creole and Cajun cultures helped create gumbo. This stew is generally made with shellfish, tomatoes, and andouille sausage. Jambalaya is a rice dish with vegetables, sausage, and seafood.

Pralines

Ask an adult to help you!

These tasty candies are a New Orleans specialty. Get a taste of Louisiana at home!

Ingredients
1 cup light brown sugar
1 cup granulated sugar
$1/2$ cup cream

$1^1/_2$ cups pecans
2 tablespoons butter

Directions
Cook the brown sugar, granulated sugar, and cream together in a saucepan over medium heat. Stir occasionally until the mixture thickens. Add the pecans and butter and continue stirring for several minutes. Once everything is melted together, remove the pan from the heat. Allow the mixture to cool for 10 minutes, then use a spoon to drop small balls of it onto waxed paper or foil. Allow the candy to cool and harden, and then enjoy!

New Orleans' French Quarter is home to buildings that date back to the 1700s.

Sights and Sounds

Louisiana offers a range of environments, from alligator-filled bayous to the historic halls of the capitol at Baton Rouge. In each and every corner of the state lies something new and different to be discovered. Good food, lively music, and exciting sports events are just the beginning. What will you explore in Louisiana? ★

Famous People

Kate Chopin

(1851–1904) was a writer who was best known for her short stories and novels about the Creole people of Louisiana.

Sidney Bechet

(1897–1959) was a saxophonist and clarinetist who helped pioneer New Orleans's unique style of jazz.

Madam C. J. Walker

(1867–1919) was a businessperson whose successful beauty products made her one of the country's first self-made female millionaires. She was born in Delta.

Truman Capote

(1924–1984) was a writer famous for books such as *In Cold Blood* and *Breakfast at Tiffany's*. He was born in New Orleans.

Fats Domino

(1928–) is a singer, songwriter, and pianist who helped pioneer rock and roll music in the 1950s. He is from New Orleans.

Kathleen Babineaux Blanco ★

(1942–) is a politician who served as the first female governor of Louisiana. She was in office from 2004 until 2008. She was born in Coteau.

Ellen DeGeneres ★

(1958–) is a comedian, actress, and television host who is best known for her popular daytime talk show. She was born in Metairie.

Emeril Lagasse

(1959–) is a world-famous chef, television personality, and restaurateur. He got his start in New Orleans and uses a traditional Louisiana cooking style.

Jared Leto

(1971–) is an actor and musician who has appeared in many TV series and films and achieved worldwide success with his rock band, 30 Seconds to Mars. He is from Bossier City.

Peyton Manning ★

(1976–) is a former NFL quarterback who holds many records and has led his teams to two Super Bowl victories. He was born in New Orleans.

Anthony Mackie

(1978–) is an actor who has appeared in many films, including the *Avengers* and *Captain America* series. He is from New Orleans.

Lil Wayne

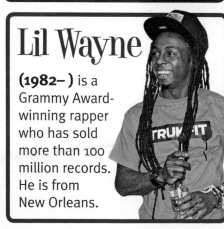

(1982–) is a Grammy Award-winning rapper who has sold more than 100 million records. He is from New Orleans.

Did You Know That . . .

The Louisiana Purchase included parts of what are now Montana, Wyoming, North Dakota, South Dakota, Minnesota, Iowa, Missouri, Nebraska, Kansas, New Mexico, Oklahoma, Texas, Arkansas, and Louisiana!

Baton Rouge is French for "red pole." The city got its name when French explorers saw a red pole that local Native American groups used to mark the edge of their hunting area.

About 450 million tons of cargo move through Louisiana's ports each year.

Louisiana covers a total of 52,375 square miles (135,651 sq km). That is more than 33 times the size of Rhode Island!

A strong French heritage lives on in Louisiana. Still today, varieties of French are spoken there, the best known being Louisiana Creole. Even the state's legal system is based on a system created by French emperor Napoleon I.

Bonjou!
Hello!

Louisiana's highest point is Driskill Mountain, at 535 feet (163 m) above sea level. Its lowest point is New Orleans, at 8 feet (2.4 m) below sea level.

Did you find the truth?

(T) Louisiana is broken into parishes rather than counties.

(F) French explorers were the first people to settle in what is now Louisiana.

Resources

Books

Nonfiction

Benoit, Peter. *Hurricane Katrina*. New York: Children's Press, 2011.

Lassieur, Allison. *Louisiana*. New York: Children's Press, 2014.

Fiction

Cochran, Thomas. *Running the Dogs*. New York: Farrar Straus Giroux, 2007.

Holt, Kimberly Willis. *My Louisiana Sky*. New York: Holt, 1998.

Rhodes, Jewell Parker. *Ninth Ward*. New York: Little, Brown and Co., 2010.

Movies

Blues Brothers 2000 (1998)

Deepwater Horizon (2016)

The Haunted Mansion (2003)

Hotel for Dogs (2009)

Sounder (1972)

Visit this Scholastic website for more information on Louisiana:
★ www.factsfornow.scholastic.com
Enter the keyword **Louisiana**

Important Words

bayous (BY-yooz) streams that run slowly through swamps and lead to or from lakes or rivers

colonize (KAH-luh-nize) to establish a new colony, or territory settled by people from another country

Creole (KREE-ohl) the language of the descendants of people who lived in Louisiana when it was a French colony

delta (DEL-tuh) an area of land shaped like a triangle where a river enters the sea

endangered (en-DAYN-jurd) in danger of becoming extinct, usually because of human activity

floodplains (FLUHD-playnz) areas of land on the sides of rivers that experience flooding when water levels are high

humidity (hyoo-MID-uh-tee) the amount of moisture in the air

mammoths (MAM-uhthz) animals that looked like large elephants, with long, curved tusks and shaggy hair

plantations (plan-TAY-shunz) large farms found in warm climates where crops such as coffee, rubber, and cotton are grown

silt (SILT) the fine particles of soil that are carried along by flowing water and that eventually settle to the bottom of a river or lake

Index

Page numbers in **bold** indicate illustrations.

About the Author

Jennifer Zeiger lives in Chicago, Illinois, where she writes and edits books for children.